Mini-Messages from
God #3

Linda K. Henderson

ROYSTON Publishing

BK Royston Publishing
Jeffersonville, IN
http://www.bkroystonpublishing.com
bkroystonpublishing@gmail.com

© Copyright – 2025

All Rights Reserved. No part of this book may be reproduced, stored in a retrieval system, or transmitted by any means without the written permission of the author.

Cover Design: Elite Book Covers

ISBN-13: 978-1-967282-11-1

King James Version (KJV) - Public Domain

New International Version (NIV) - Holy Bible, New International Version®, NIV® Copyright ©1973, 1978, 1984, 2011 by Biblica, Inc.® Used by permission. All rights reserved worldwide.

New King James Version (NKJV) - Scripture taken from the New King James Version®. Copyright © 1982 by Thomas Nelson. Used by permission. All rights reserved.

Printed in the United States of America

Dedication

I dedicate this third book as the finished part of a triptych, to my husband, family, friends, and supporters. God has truly blessed my life. Most importantly, I give my Heavenly Father the glory in all things. There is nothing I can do better than He can. My goal is to please Him and allow Him to use me and allow others to see His work in and through me. To God be the glory, in Jesus' name. Amen.

Acknowledgements

Once again, in appreciation to all who have supported, who came through in the nick of time. I thank all who passed on Mini Messages from God, sharing my application of the Word of God to family and friends. I acknowledge all who encouraged and prayed for me throughout this undertaking, asking for more, really enjoying the process with me. I love you all.

TABLE OF CONTENTS

Dedication	iii
Acknowledgements	iv
TRIPTYCH	vii
By Faith	1
Go God's Way	5
Ask God!	11
Hindrance	19
Praise Him!	25
Thank You, Lord	29
What Have I Missed?	33
Endurance	39
Make the Right Choice	45
A Time for Restoration	51
Legacy, What We Leave Behind	57
A Brother's Love	63
Yes, I Am Saved	65
What He Said	71

Shade	75
Accused	81
The Secret Place	87
Take A Stand	93
Persevere	99
Get Your House In Order	105
About the Author	111
More Books by Linda K. Henderson	112

TRIPTYCH

A set of three associated, artistic, literary, or musical works intended to be appreciated together.

This third book, Mini Messages from God #3, is considered the last piece of the triptych. These literary pieces make up a part of my journey with Christ. They are linked together to depict a period of learning, who the Trinity was and how God the Father, God the Son and God the Spirit fit together. The application of the Word of God affected and inspired my walk; they can also inspire you as well.

This is an opportunity to touch lives and pass on my experiences and insight into His purpose and plan for me. It is learning how God loves me more than anyone else can, that He is on our side and His whole intent is to get us and keep us with Him.

I hope you see the love of God in each message. Life can sometimes be hard, but He is there. Life may be stressful, but He carries our load. Life is wonderful when you can see, understand, draw nearer, and let Him lead the way. I encourage you all to pass these messages along and allow others the chance to go on their own journey with Christ.

BY FAITH

Scripture: Romans 10:17 (KJV)
"So, then faith cometh by hearing, and hearing by the word of God."

By faith, we withstood the test of time, learning and growing, striving to stay true to our values.

By faith, we worked and fought to walk worthy of Your Word; we have stood the test of time.

By faith, we received Your plan to restore, to grow, and to shine our light where we are planted.

By faith, we love and believe in You, God. No, man can go for us; we must.

By faith, wisdom is given when we ask, helping us all to complete our tasks.

By faith, we follow Jesus, striving to do our best and continuing our journey.

We stand in Jesus' name—by faith.

REFLECTION

_____
_____
_____
_____
_____
_____
_____
_____
_____
_____
_____
_____
_____
_____

REFLECTION

_____

_____

_____

_____

_____

_____

_____

_____

_____

_____

_____

_____

_____

GO THE WAY OF CHRIST

Scripture: John 14:6 (KJV)

"Jesus saith unto him, I am the way, the truth and the life: no man cometh unto the Father, but by me."

Anyone aspiring to be used by God must accept responsibility by searching for or seeking out His plan for how He sees things and wants things done. He instructs us on how to accomplish what He desires. Moses struck the rock and still, the water flowed. God is faithful to His plan. God wanted the Israelites to see His kindness, patience He had with them, and provision for them no matter what. By not following the instructions or being obedient to God's will,

Moses was essentially out of line. He was responsible for people missing God's sentiment and His intent.

Moses's stunning attempt to exact satisfaction by striking the rock instead of speaking to it did not accomplish God's purpose.

Accordingly, there were consequences to his action. God's appeal to the people was love, not meant to be harsh but to show His heart toward them. God was coordinating the Israelites' experience so they would understand just what they meant to Him, trust Him with their well-being and their very lives.

The power of God is on display as His provision accomplishes His plan. There is a difference He wanted to make to lead them to the next level of trust, faith, and understanding. God's way is still the best way for us today. Letting our emotions get the best of us is not choosing life in a situation. The people frustrated Moses, leading him not to enter into the Promised Land. What a pain to miss God; the outcome was not His plan.

We, as God's people, must up our game, not stop too soon, and complete the task. It can be overwhelming to follow God's plan and deal with stiff-necked people. Moses had prayed and interceded for the people the entire way. He had to put aside his fears and insecurities to even approach the Pharaoh. Moses had purposed in himself to do as his father had asked. It was a significant hardship for him, yet he persevered.

Like Moses, Abraham fought to do the right thing in God's sight, and there were barriers there as well. As ambassadors of Christ, we will face the same challenges and miss God's purpose for our ministries. However, God continues to pursue us and use us for His glory, not so that we can be seen, but so that His love will be evident. God loves us all. Because Jesus came, God views us through the sacrifices He made. We all have ministries, whether good or evil, we must choose. We are not all perfect, but some moments are perfect in time. God loves His creation; He said it was good, and even the angels wonder why.

Prayer: Help us, Lord, not to become weary with well doing. We have been there and done that. It is not wise for us to not follow You. I thank You because love is the foundation that You build on. Thank You for seeing us for who we are. In Jesus' name. Amen.

REFLECTION

ASK GOD!

Scripture: Matthew 7:7-12 (KJV)
"Ask, and it shall be given you; seek, and ye shall find; knock, and it shall be opened unto you."

It is coming; God will not have us ignorant of the enemy's devices, or His plan and purpose. Satan wants to be God and is an imitator. Choose life, not death; love, not hate; blessings, not curses. Young and old choose life in every situation, make the right choice, and when we miss it, there is no guilt, just an opportunity to ask God for direction. There is no shame. Just go before God, get it right with Him, and ask Him to put you on the road to the everlasting, to check you out, and make sure that there is no evil way keeping you from eternity. And move on.

God gives us our choices. He makes and shows us the way. We need only to follow His will. We should not listen to anyone else or any other voice. When shame, guilt, and doubt come about, that is the enemy. He is not your father. God said that we are the head and not the tail, above only and not beneath. We are part of a royal priesthood. We are the light of the world and the salt of the earth. That is who we are, and much more.

Our Father said what He has made is good. So, if there is any other voice that is not of your Father, you do not have to listen to someone else's father. Do you?

Furthermore, you do not have to believe it. We are not guilty, nor are we ashamed; we are the children of the Most-High God. We have His grace and opportunity, because of Jesus' redemption, not to be slaves to sin and believe the enemy's lies. We must endeavor to pray, intercede, and ask God for ourselves on our family's behalf. We must apply the Word to our lives first. We must listen for God's direction and listen for His voice. We must listen for His love and recognize that we are loved and that we belong to Him. For real. For life. He will not stop guiding us or teaching us till Jesus comes back. Form a close relationship with God.

Call out your children's names. Push them in the right direction. Teach them about God. Recognize their gifts and talents as they grow. Lead them in the right direction. We are always talking about how old we are. We should close our eyes and look at our young selves, our fit selves, our running and speaking selves, being an example at home and work. We should strive to see ourselves as God sees us. Consider Abraham having children at 100 years old, like Sarah, who was barren but was made whole. Look at Moses, still strong, clear eyesight. Look at Ruth and Boaz; see yourself in them. With regards to what you have been asking for, do not give up. Revisit your prayers from your youth. See yourself renewed as the eagles.

Get ready, act today, send cards and letters, and build new relationships. If you have tried and nothing happens, it's time to move on. We must ask, and God will help us move forward and reach our goals. The ones He has put in place for us will encourage us, and He will rain down the blessing that He has kept for us. Remember who we are and who He is in our lives. Come on, young people, in spirit of God, mount up on wings as eagles, run and do not get weary, walk, and do not faint. Isaiah 40:31

Prayer: Rain down your blessings upon us and wash away the old. Renew our strength as the eagles in Jesus' name. Thank You, Lord, for the youthful zest and zeal that keeps us asking, seeking, and knocking. Winning souls forever in Jesus' name. Amen

REFLECTION

_____

_____

_____

_____

_____

_____

_____

_____

_____

_____

_____

_____

_____

_____

REFLECTION

HINDRANCE

Scripture: Galatians 5:7 (NKJV)
"You ran well. Who hindered you from obeying the truth?"

The definition of a hindrance is a thing that provides resistance, delay, or obstruction to something or someone's development or progress. The Word asks, "Who hindered you?" Well, we can be a hindrance to ourselves, but the enemy often orchestrates it through us, our family, or a friend. A person's will can get in the way of our dreams, our mission, or our purpose. Others can hold us back because their problems seem more significant than ours, and sometimes, they are. However, the enemy will use who he can.

When you are at your most vulnerable, the enemy will use the circumstance at hand to take advantage of you and use you for his gain. That is why the Word instructs us to examine ourselves. Have you? Ask God to examine you and show you if there is anything that He needs to change. Do not be used by the devil or lean to your understanding. There are issues that we cannot manage or need to attend to ourselves. We have all made mistakes by following someone and believing in their wisdom when the evidence is contrary to it. When people look upon your life, they should see your good works and glorify God.

Good works are necessary, accompanied by faith. Everyone has missions provided by God—not you. Precious children of God, do not fall for the devices of the enemy; we began well, but what have we left behind or forgotten? Pick up the Word of God and look at the truth. A little knowledge without wisdom or correct application can be extremely dangerous to you and others. In Galatians, they ran the race well; however, there is always a trap set by the enemy. Be careful and watch where you step. There may be no coming back unscathed.

Prayer: Thank You, Lord, for instructions and for not having us ignorant of the enemies' devices. Thank You for not letting the enemy use us against each other. In Jesus' name. Amen

REFLECTION

_____
_____
_____
_____
_____
_____
_____
_____
_____
_____
_____
_____
_____
_____
_____
_____

REFLECTION

_____

_____

_____

_____

_____

_____

_____

_____

_____

_____

_____

_____

_____

_____

PRAISE HIM!

Scripture: Psalms 150:1-6 (KJV)
"For the spirit of heaviness put on the garment of praise."

Depression, guilt, shame, and condemnation are spirits of heaviness. When Jesus came, we were absolved of all of that, and grace was instituted on our behalf. Praising God is our way of escape and a weapon to avoid the enemy's attempts to corrupt God's plan in our lives. So, praise God for His goodness, forgiveness, mercy, and grace. Praise Him when things are going well and when they are not. Praise Him for who He is and who we are in Him.

Whatever burdens you and makes you feel unnecessary, praise God. Praise Him for always working on our behalf and remember His faithfulness and the protection plan He has for us. Consider His love towards us. Remind Him of the many promises to us. Receive Him as your best friend; He is closer than a brother.

Our action of praising fulfills our responsibility; heaviness cannot survive in the presence of praise, not just from your mouth, but from your heart—a heart where the furrow ground has been plowed up. The hardness is broken down, leaving only fertile ground where your fruit can flourish and remain. The enemy can oppress us by using depression against us. It is an excellent tool of the enemy to keep you feeling guilty and not seeking or asking our Father for help in all aspects of your life. The spirit of heaviness can leave a significant chasm for us to navigate if we have not given it to God. He tells us in I Peter 5:7, to cast our cares on Him, for He cares for us.

Prayer: Thank You for covering us and for the garment of praise, so that we can live in confidence and certainty of Your love. Thank You for being willing to show us Your way and be with us always. Thanks for having our back, in Jesus' name. Amen.

REFLECTION

_____

_____

_____

_____

_____

_____

_____

_____

_____

_____

_____

_____

_____

THANK YOU, LORD!

Scripture: I Thessalonians 5:18-22 (KJV)
"Whenever we do not know what to do, we know it is God's will that we give thanks."

Thank you, Lord, that we depend on You.

Thank you, Lord, for instructing us in all we do.

Thank you, Lord, for Your love and correction.

For showing us Your precise directions.

Thanks for life and love and your awesome splendor.

Nothing can compare to what Your Word has created.

You spoke, and I was.

You breathed, and I live.

Without You I cannot see.

Your hand created in me all You called me to be.

Let us all rejoice and receive the glory of God.

I thank You, Lord, in the good times and the bad; in abundance and while abased.

Prayer: Thank You, Lord, for giving us grace. In Jesus' name. Amen

REFLECTION

_____

_____

_____

_____

_____

_____

_____

_____

_____

_____

_____

_____

_____

_____

ENDURANCE

Scripture: 2 Timothy-4:3-4 (KJV)

"For the time will come when they will not endure sound doctrine, but after their lusts shall they heap to themselves teachers, having itching ears; and they shall turn away their ears from the truth and shall be turned into fables."

In Leviticus 10:1-10, it discusses Aaron's sons. Both took their censors and incense and offered fire that was strange or unfamiliar fire to God. The fire was not sanctioned by God. They lost their very lives. So, there will come a time when some will want it their way. They think that it will work for what they are doing, so they offer up something to God that is not the truth. The strange fire pertains to the ways of doing things, the ways of thinking, usurping the role of leadership, and thinking we know better. When we do not hold onto the truth, we cannot endure God's process. We go looking elsewhere for ways that work for us.

Whether in our homes, workplaces, or churches, rules and regulations are in place, and we should follow them to the best of our ability. If you have not noticed, most things in the Word of God are established for everyone to be taught and grow. So, we, who are in the church, must be ready to go out into the world in the name of Jesus. So, the teaching brings us all into agreement.

Endurance is taking a stand, not leaning to our understanding, but asking God for help in the name of Jesus. People are sitting in the same seats, not growing, still thinking, and doing as the world does. We are not ready when people cannot look at our lives and give God the glory. People must see the difference in your life; just because you attend church is not enough. By establishing a relationship with God for yourself, speaking and listening to your Father in Heaven, and using His Son's name as a cheat code by His Spirit, you are set up for success. Hallelujah! If you are out there listening (or reading), come and join our mission to build the Kingdom of God. We have a great team. Get to know who is working on your behalf every day. Get to know who never sleeps or slumbers. You do not have to worry or be anxious for anything. Put your hand in His.

When you choose Christ, you will be on the right team. There will still be battles to fight, corrections to make, and choices to be made so that our lives will not fall apart. You will still need to stand and remain faithful, trusting in God. We know the end of the story—WE WIN!

Prayer: Thank You, Lord, that Your Word says we can run and not get weary, walk, and not faint as we wait and continue serving You. Thank You for endurance and the truth. In Jesus' name. Amen.

REFLECTION

REFLECTION

WHAT HAVE I MISSED?

Scripture: Luke 1:13, 16-17 (KJV)
"Zechariah could not believe...Gabriel struck him deaf and mute until the day his son was born."

Zechariah's son was John the Baptist. Zechariah could not believe that he and his wife, Elizabeth, would have a child at their age. In the story of Zechariah, we find he was the only participant who disagreed with what the angel had spoken to him. First, he and his wife thought they were too old, and then the name God had chosen was not customary for Zechariah. He wanted a family name, so he missed out on the blessing of the whole event. Finally, his mouth was shut, so he would not speak contrary to God's word. In essence, Zechariah was deaf and dumb until his son, John the Baptist, was born. In the end, Zechariah did praise God.

Looking back, we can see the things we missed along the way. As children of the Most-High God, we should ask Him what we have overlooked in our journey. As seniors, mothers, fathers, sisters, brothers, friends, and family, we need to take a moment to ask God: Did I make a wrong turn? Some things did not go as planned. We did not arrive when we thought we should. Did we forget to ask God? What have we missed? Was it love, compassion, or forgiveness? Have we received His grace and mercy? Have we boldly grabbed hold of His promises and His forgiveness, His acceptance and His adoption? Ask yourself: Have I judged others too harshly? Did I prolong my journey and misread the instructions? Did I pay more attention to the opinions of men and women and fail to demonstrate God's will? Did my GPS reroute me or was my music too loud and distracting me from my course?

Have you ever been late to the party and wondered what you missed? We need to catch up and get with the program. So, let us get ready and ask God to reroute us.

Father God, today, we come boldly to reflect, to remember, and be reminded of Your Word, to regroup, and to be rerouted, if need be. We come today to ask for guidance for perfect peace, knowing that if

You were to come today, we would be ready. Amen.

On occasion, we are like Zechariah and are held back for a while until God's will is done. The great news is that God will bless us. He may take over to save us, but like Zechariah, who had a son to raise and was able to see the great things John the Baptist was slated to do, God's plan will come through for us. What are you slated to do? Ask God for His plan, and let go?

Prayer: Thank You, Lord, for saying that Your way is the best! Because of Jesus, your grace is sufficient. We praise You for our position in You. We praise You for Your love for us and for the fact that You are waiting for us to come before You. In Jesus' name. Amen.

REFLECTION

_____

_____

_____

_____

_____

_____

_____

_____

_____

_____

_____

_____

_____

_____

MAKE THE RIGHT CHOICE

Scripture: Deuteronomy 30:19 (KJV)
"I have set before your life and death, you choose…"

God has put before us life and death. We must choose life. We have been given the opportunity to decide how our lives will go. We can be obedient to the Word of God or our way of thinking. The scriptures refer to it as leaning to our understanding. The only caveat is that He tells us which one to choose: "Choose Life."

Choose life in your relationships, friendships, work relationships, and even in your community. Do not let your way dictate who you are. Choose your words wisely. Do not let your emotions cause you to speak words that cannot be taken back. Once they are spoken, they cannot be retrieved. Speak life and not death, blessings and not curses, love and not hate. These are life choices. This includes social media, texting, and messaging. Furthermore, any form of AI communication is included. Technology is new to some of us, but our Father in Heaven already knew what was in store at this time. Choose a life of financial stability by saving and avoiding unnecessary spending. Give! And it shall be given unto you! Luke 6:38

God says we cannot serve Him and mammon. The love of money is of the enemy when we love it more than God. The Greek word for mammon in scripture is "mammonas," which can mean money, material wealth, or the portrayal of riches as a false idol worthy of our time and devotion. Satan influences us to love money and riches. Rich people sometimes struggle to make good choices with their money. They often need to take care of some priorities but spend money on other things instead. People cheat and steal to have more. Those with money usually find many evil things to do with it. You know, drugs and trafficking, stealing from the poor to achieve more power. They become money-hungry and power-hungry. Others are so jealous that they fall into the pit that they have dug.

God has given us a choice, and we are not His robots but created for His good pleasure. Money is one of the greatest struggles for us as His children. The Word says, "It will be harder for a rich man to get to heaven than a camel going through the eye of a needle." When we make a habit of giving, it will be given unto us; that is a promise. God promises to take care of all our needs. So, make the right choice. Choose life in your spiritual growth. We must not become stuck by failing to hear what God has to say. Make the change, intentionally grow, and get understanding and wisdom from God. Are we doing the same thing repeatedly? Lord, help us move away from the milk of the Word so we can have some meat and grow thereby. Leaders are not exempt, and some will not be moved by the Word of God. They will not heed His warnings. God forgives us if we ask, accept Jesus as His son, and believe He rose again. However, making an ungodly choice makes our lives significantly more difficult.

Prayer: Help us, Lord! In Jesus' name.

REFLECTION

_____

_____

_____

_____

_____

_____

_____

_____

_____

_____

_____

_____

_____

_____

A TIME FOR RESTORATION

Scripture: Proverbs 6:31 (KJV)
"But if he be found, he shall restore sevenfold:"

This is a time for the restoration of relationships, putting the past behind us, and moving forward into a higher calling and a more enlightened way of thinking. Repairs will be made, and parts that are broken will be fixed. If you receive forgiveness, you must forgive. Matthew 6:9-13 (KJV)

It is easier said than done; even so, it is a must. Relationships and trust may not be the same ever again. We may feel betrayed and struggle to place the past, the hurts, and all the careless words in Jesus's hand. Let His will be done, not ours.

We have all, in some form or fashion, experienced a breakup, a betrayal by someone we did not see coming, whether it was a boyfriend, best friend, husband, wife, or a work relationship.

When your very being has been called into question, your spiritual relationship with God and your character are maligned, misrepresented, or misunderstood. When you find you cannot trust someone to be a confidante, this is a job for our God. Although you may not see a way out or a resolution, God knows and is not surprised; He has our best interests at heart.

It is a spiritual battle we fight that is not against flesh and blood. Peter was constantly telling Jesus what would or would not happen. Jesus said, "Get thee behind me Satan." It was a spiritual battle, and Satan will use anyone or anything. Let the Lord handle the problem, and while we retrieve our spiritual confidence, God will return to us what has been stolen, taken, or snatched away.

Job received twice what he lost: more children, finances, cattle, and sheep. He grew closer to God, his friends learned that they had given bad advice, and his wife learned the best lesson of all. When God allowed the restoration of all that was lost, she witnessed God moving on their behalf. Although she had lost all faith, she was blessed, nevertheless. All of them had an opportunity for restoration. So do we, in Jesus' name.

Prayer: Thank You, Lord, for allowing us to see and know You in our daily situations. Thank You for letting the dried-up things in our lives be revived and for letting these dry bones stand up and take their rightful place. In Jesus Christ's name. Amen.

REFLECTION

_____

_____

_____

_____

_____

_____

_____

_____

_____

_____

_____

_____

_____

_____

_____

REFLECTION

LEGACY, WHAT WE LEAVE BEHIND

Scripture: Hebrews 11:8 (NIV)
"By faith Abraham, when called to go to a place he would later receive as his inheritance, obeyed, and went even though he did not know where he was going."

Abraham believed God and received an inheritance, a legacy to leave behind. He decided to be obedient to God and face the unknown. He was considered faithful by God, and it was accounted to him as righteousness.

We are the righteousness of God in Christ Jesus. When we are afraid, as Abraham was, we can trust God to lead us into the promised land. We can trust him to keep us even in the midst of fear. Although Abraham was afraid, he did it anyway. He was faithful, righteous, and believed in God; therefore, he trusted Him implicitly to be with him. So should we.

Everything we need is documented in the pages of the Bible; all life and death decisions are there. Abraham left these things as a legacy. The world has adopted and changed some of the wisdom of God's words into a distorted context. We are His righteousness and should be able to rightly divide the word of truth, enabling us to discern the difference between right and wrong.

We hinder our progress, as Abraham did, when he took his nephew, Lot, with him. Sometimes, we must leave people behind because God knows the outcome. Lot significantly slowed down Abraham's progression. It was not just one person; Abraham's wife and children, herdsman, guards, and even servants were with him, causing conflict between Abraham and Lot's people.

Nevertheless, Abraham received and was known as the father of many nations.

Methuselah and Noah are part of Abraham's family history, as were Isaac and Jacob after him. Look at your heritage across several generations and consider the future to envision what your legacy can be. We inherited the promises of Abraham as righteous children of God in Christ Jesus.

In the natural, we may not know about our past or who our natural relatives are. We can explore Ancestry.com, another website, or we can get a DNA sample. However, we have been adopted into Jesus' lineage, and it includes promises made by God. We have a legacy through Jesus Christ.

Prayer: Thank You, Father, that we are not unsure of where we come from or where we are headed. Praise to You for our adoption and righteousness in Christ Jesus. Thank You for seeing our troubles and mistakes and loving us anyway. In Jesus' name. Amen

REFLECTION

_____

_____

_____

_____

_____

_____

_____

_____

_____

_____

_____

_____

_____

_____

_____

A BROTHER'S LOVE

A brother's love will stand the test of time.

They grow stronger as they stand in line.

Waiting for wisdom that only God can give.

Showing them His plan as they live.

A brother's love was always meant to be.

To hold fast no matter how far each went.

Knowing the bond only they perceive and the height they alone would achieve.

The heart only knows the love they shared and how much they cared.

A brother's love in Jesus' name.

REFLECTION

YES! I AM SAVED

Scripture: Revelation 12:11 (KJV)
"Overcame by the blood of the Lamb and by the word of their testimony."

We often struggle to know who we are. Jesus came and took on our sins. We must be reminded time and time again that we have been redeemed by the blood of the lamb. He did it for us so we would not have to take it on ourselves. Jesus set us free, and we are. Repeat after me: "Yes, I am saved."

Testimony

Gideon had to be reminded that he was a mighty man of valor. God chose him and reminded him of his courage and strength, as well as his chosen and anointed status. Yet, he could not grasp the concepts of who God said he was. We fear and let what others do or say dictate who we are. If anyone asks, please say, "Yes, I am saved." Do not be surprised if you find yourself in a predicament, questioning and wondering what you need to do and where you need to go. It is pointless if you do not believe what Jesus did for you. When you seek the Lord with your whole heart, strive to live as He has instructed. You are halfway there; once you begin to ask, seek, and knock, your confidence returns, and you can reply unequivocally, "Yes, I am saved."

We must not position ourselves to forget who our God is and what He did for us. We do not have to pray and beg for forgiveness—we are forgiven. We are saved and set apart unto God. We cannot get stuck and struggle to move forward. We must believe in God, trust in Him, have faith in Him, and do as He asks so that we are safe in Him. YES, YOU ARE SAVED!

Prayer: Father, we come before You, saved and redeemed. We repent of any wicked ways and ask You to send us on to everlasting. Help us get it right. Help us to be humble and filled with gratitude. Thank You for giving us all we need: wisdom, understanding, and knowledge of You, dear Father. You sent Your precious Spirit to order our steps in the ways of Jesus Christ. Rebuke, correct, and comfort us in Jesus' name. Amen

REFLECTION

REFLECTION

_____

_____

_____

_____

_____

_____

_____

_____

_____

_____

_____

_____

_____

WHAT HE SAID!

Scripture: 1 Cor. 2:1 (KJV)
"And I, brethren, when I came to you, came not with excellency of speech or wisdom, declaring unto you the testimony of God."

Paul wanted the Corinthians to know that he did not use big words or that his wisdom was not of worldly ways; instead, it was what he knew of Jesus. Paul said what He said. Paul was fearful and extremely nervous. However, Paul demonstrated as he preached in the power of the Spirit of God. Paul did not just talk; the power of God emanated from him. In Romans 4:6, Paul stated that he wanted to tell the people that he could not boast about himself or take the glory. Jesus was crucified for us. Paul said what Jesus said. When they were weak, he stood by them. He never left them as Jesus proclaimed. Paul did not follow or listen to the teachings of the other disciples, except for the message of Jesus' crucifixion. As others discussed who had baptized them and professed allegiance to Peter or the other disciples, Paul was content that he had only preached and taught what Jesus had told him. He spoke about the new converts and those who were left out at the beginning.

The Gentiles were specifically to whom Paul was called. He was given instruction straight from Jesus, from heaven. The false prophets were causing confusion among the new converts, leading to division within each congregation. The Jews wanted to keep everything the same and have the new converts follow Jewish traditions. Paul knew differently, and he wrote letters and visited Corinth, Ephesus, and other New Christians to keep them on the same page.

Prayer: Thank You, Lord, for the adoption, Your grace and that we were invited in and receive Your mercy, along with the inheritance that Abraham was promised. Thank You, Lord, for Your sacrifices and, above all, Your love. In Jesus' name, Amen.

REFLECTION

SHADE

Scripture: Jonah 4:4-6 (KJV)
"And the Lord God prepared a gourd...to give him shade...to deliver him from grief."

Scripture: Ephesians 4:25 (NIV)
"Therefore, each of you must put off falsehood and speak truthfully to your neighbor, for we are all members of one body."

Do you really know the truth? The things that we let come out of our mouths, as well as our social media, texts, and tweets, can be shocking. A word used in the world today by young and old alike is, 'shade.' The world uses shade when someone is being judgmental, they think everything goes.

However, the shade that God provides imparts truth or wisdom. God's shade may seem common to some and often outweighs common sense. Everything is not for us—children of God. Just because everyone is doing it, wearing it, saying it, dating it, or even smoking it, does not mean it is profitable for you or the body of Christ.

Samson was told not to let a razor come near his hair. He was also told not to drink. There are specifications that God gives us individually and collectively. God has a plan! When parents or grandparents provide you with advice or correct you, it is not to harm or hurt you. It is to give you wisdom. Samson's mother was given the instructions concerning him, and she was responsible for passing them on to him, not judging him or throwing shade, but sowing wisdom into him. Samson got off track; was able to complete his mission, but he made his life more treacherous than it should have been. He was still one of the Bible's superheroes and an example for us all.

Yes, we can do as we see fit; however, if God's way is not considered, we will end up going too far out of the way and staying too long. Furthermore, it will cost you more than you ever intended to spend and could cause your time, finances, and GPS to be rerouted. The 'shade' that the world attributes to your sensibility is only a covering for you, for the child, the friend, or the family. All of us have had 'shade' applied to us, specifically lies, half-truths, and misunderstandings. Why are we surprised? Jesus was the first recipient of the world's 'shade.' Know the difference between the two. The world's shade is not God's wisdom. Do not be deceived. Know the truth, and the truth will set you free.

Prayer: Thank You, Lord, for Your mercy, grace, wisdom, understanding, and knowledge. Help us to know the difference between Your ways and the ways of the world. In Jesus' name. Amen.

REFLECTION

_____

_____

_____

_____

_____

_____

_____

_____

_____

_____

_____

_____

_____

_____

REFLECTION

_____

_____

_____

_____

_____

_____

_____

_____

_____

_____

_____

_____

_____

_____

ACCUSED

Scripture: Matthew 27:12 (KJV)
"And when he was accused of the chief priests and elders, he answered nothing."

Jesus said *'nothing,'* for us, how hard is that? He did not defend Himself; He did not quote the scripture that they should have known. He did not explain Himself. Jesus answered not a word. He did not call angels from heaven to save Him. He remained silent.

Have you ever felt like the lady who was accused and judged by the crowd as she was dragged out before Jesus? The accusations were sure to get her stoned. She was a lady who had the attention of many men, yet she was the only one accused. Jesus said to the rowdy people, "If you have no sin, then cast the first stone." Then He wrote in the sand, and as He wrote, one by one, the accusers left. Jesus said to the lady, "Where are your accusers?" They were gone. Finally, He said to her, "Go and sin no more." Have you ever been the accused?

When we are accused, oh my, what a struggle to keep quiet, not to retaliate, or to plan to do tit for tat. It is hard, and we are tempted to set the accusers straight. We want to tell them off or to throw a few punches. How dare they say what they said and do what they did? Jesus, on the other hand, had done nothing. He committed no sin. Jesus was completing the plan for us, standing in for us because of our sins. Wow! Jesus took it all on Himself.

We are not perfect, but He is. We were guilty, but He was not. We have options because of Him. Thank You, Jesus, for not denying us but forgiving us. Jesus knows the pain of accusations; He knows the truth, yet He let it go. Things are unfair, but where are your accusers? Jesus knows your past, and His blood took care of those things. Jesus was accused Himself, so He knows where we are coming from. The accusers knew they were guilty themselves of the same sin. It gave them something to think about.

No one told the lady caught in the midst of sin that they were sorry or that they were wrong. When people reach through the blood of Jesus to accuse, they are in dangerous territory. The covering and the washing away of our sins took place by the sacrificial, cleansing blood of Jesus. The enemy is the accuser of the brethren. Do not let him catch you up in being an accuser, too. Be kind to one another, forgive whether anyone says sorry or not, and most importantly, love one another anyway.

Prayer: Thank You, Lord, for Your sacrifice, love, and grace. Help us not to fall in with the enemy's plan. Help us to be true-blue friends. In Jesus' name. Amen.

REFLECTION

REFLECTION

THE SECRET PLACE

Scripture: Psalm 91:1 (KJV)
"He that dwelleth in the secret place of the Most-High God shall abide under the shadow of the Almighty."

Let this be one of the greatest reminders for you: run to the secret place, which is the Most-High God. In troubled times, seek God. Before you call a friend or go on social media, seek God. He knows our problems, the situations, or circumstances, and also has the answers. He is our source in all things. We must make Him our dwelling place no matter where we are. He never sleeps or slumbers; He is a phone call away, and even without a charge, He can always be reached because He is our refuge.

Jesus is always our protection in every area. He is someone we can hide behind; we are safe there, under the shadow of His wings. We can trust in Him. He is our deliverer from all evil, from any enemy, the noisome pestilence, and whatever anyone is saying and doing. Tests from the enemy are of your faith in the Word of God. Hold onto God during tests; He is our keeper. The results of God's protection are that there is no fear of what comes at night or noonday, nor terror and destruction in darkness. You cannot be afraid of the political landscape or worldly tragedies. Stay close to your protector so you are reminded of what His Word says. He has the heart of the king in His hand. There are assurances for believers dwelling in the secret place.

Daniel and the three Hebrew boys stayed true to their God, and as they went through the fire. On one occasion, Daniel slept in the lions' den. Throughout their ordeal, they were saved, did not smell like smoke, and emerged from what the enemy meant for evil. Instead, God turned everything around for their good. He did it for them and He will do it for us. In Jesus' name.

Prayer: Thank You, Lord, for Your reminder; thank You for protection, care, and salvation. Thank You for continual assurance of Your deliverance. Thank You for keeping us in all Your ways. In Jesus' name. Amen.

REFLECTION

REFLECTION

_____

_____

_____

_____

_____

_____

_____

_____

_____

_____

_____

_____

_____

TAKE A STAND

Scripture: 1 Samuel 17:26 (KJV)
"And David spake to the men that stood by him, saying, what shall be done to the man that killeth this Philistine, and taketh away the reproach from Israel? for who is this uncircumcised Philistine, that he should defy the armies of the living God?"

David asked, "Who is this uncircumcised Philistine to defy the king's army?" Goliath was a giant of a man, defiant and disrespectful of God's army, led by King Saul. If we remember the circumstances, Samuel, by God's authority, chose David to be the next King. However, it would have to be after Saul's death and not announced to anyone but David's family. David was a young man, a sheep keeper for his father, and even his father was doubtful about his ability to be king. Yet here he was, effectively drawing a line in the sand and challenging a giant that dared come against the army of the Lord.

Do you men and women of God, children of the Most-High God, have any giants standing in your way? Liars or betrayers, haters, ruthless people who defy your trust. If so, it is time to draw a line in the sand and take a stand as David did. You might be tempted to hide like Saul and his army. David had fought and won battles against a lion and a bear with his slingshot and stones, he was protecting the sheep. How much more would he fight for his God?

Our obligation is only to cast our cares on God, not stones. He will take care of the rest. He cares for us and will fight our battles. Love is the principal thing. Praying for those who despitefully use and persecute us and bless those who curse us is how God would have His children react. The same victory David received with his stones is the same we shall receive with our prayers. Do not try to get them back or defend yourself. Take a stand, stand your ground, draw that line in the sand, do not cross it, and do not allow the enemy into your territory. Call on the name of Jesus and you will be saved.

Prayer: Father, God, thank You for setting the record straight for us and for not allowing the enemy's will to supersede Yours. Thank You for loving us and sending Your Word to help us. In Jesus' name. Amen.

REFLECTION

_____
_____
_____
_____
_____
_____
_____
_____
_____
_____
_____
_____
_____
_____
_____

REFLECTION

_____

_____

_____

_____

_____

_____

_____

_____

_____

_____

_____

_____

_____

PERSEVERE

Scripture: Hebrews 10:36 (NIV)
"You need to persevere so that when you have done the will of God, you will receive what is promised."

Guys, life can be difficult at times; we have all experienced it. My mother would say, "If you don't know, live long enough, and you will." Different situations warrant different solutions. One constant is our Lord and Savior, Jesus Christ, our redeemer, our promise maker, and keeper. He always remains the same, pushing us forward when we want to go back and makes a way of escape for us at every turn. He is our way maker, our promise keeper, and a light in the darkness. He is the one who hears and answers prayers. Our quality of life depends on how we receive and achieve His direction and commands. He rains grace on the just as well as the unjust, so there are many instances that we do not know or understand. Despite our attempts and efforts to get it right, Jesus moves us forward.

Perseverance is a key component in the successful fulfillment of God's will. Consider Joseph, who was despised by his brothers and sold into slavery. They were jealous of his position in his father's heart. Joseph persevered through prison, being lied on, and many hurtful situations that would stop most of us in our tracks. God ushered him forward into his destiny. Joseph moved forward despite whatever was occurring. After all, there is an enemy that distracts and thrives on imitating God with His plans for you. During the famine, Joseph became the lifeline for his family and many others.

God has a plan and promises for all of us. We may not have the lead role; however, whatever our part, it is valuable to the world. People are watching you, which makes a bigger impression than anything you say. They see your perseverance and believe that God will help them, too. Through the grace of God, we see our purpose, have the opportunity, and are granted eternal life. To God be the glory.

Prayer: Thank You, Father, for Your precious Son's grace and Your Holy Spirit—our constant companion and helper. Thank You for Your love, goodness, and mercy. In Jesus' name, I pray. Amen.

REFLECTION

REFLECTION

GET YOUR HOUSE IN ORDER

Scripture: Proverbs 27:23-24 (NKJV)
"Be diligent to know the state of your flocks. And attend to your herds:
For riches are not forever..."

Hi guys, as I sit here making calls, paying bills, and getting my files ready for tax time, I am reminded of what God says in His Word about our affairs and preparing them. He tells us to be diligent and look after our stuff. We may not have herds and flocks in our neck of the woods, but we have different things to look after.

We must start making plans today. I was happy to see the prophet Isaiah when he told Hezekiah, "Get your house in order." Also, in Proverbs, the Word says, "Be diligent to know the state of your stuff (paraphrased)." He says tomorrow is not promised, so do not go building bigger barns. Do you have a plan for giving to others and helping those less fortunate than you? The Word says what you do for the least of them, you do it unto Me (Jesus). Plan and resolve the state of your affairs now.

Start today. Ask the Holy Spirit for help in everyday life. Jesus sent Him; He will help. My home needs painting and repairs, and I have items to donate and throw away. I also have papers from previous years that need to be stored or discarded. We accumulate so many things over the years, and as we get older, it becomes too much to handle. These are the practical things, the Spirit of God will inspire us to do, or find what we need.

As for our spiritual life, it is even more important. We cannot hold onto the old way of thinking. If we want to progress in the natural, the spiritual must progress too. Instead of merely discussing, hearing, and reading the Word of God, a conscious effort must be made to apply it to our daily lives spiritually.

We must do it. Examine yourself, make sure you have faith, and trust that God has your back. Ask Him to check you out and ensure you are on the right road to everlasting life. God wants us to prove Him amazing. He wants us to ask big and pray for our desires and needs, small or large. Do not put confidence in the world or how you always do things. Do not lean to your own understanding. Call on the name of Jesus.

Prayer: Thank You, Lord, for Your help with all that concerns us. Help us, Lord, move on to Your next assignment. Free us of clutter and things that are not profitable to our lives. Thank You for the opportunity to get it right and get rid of some stuff. In Jesus' name. Amen.

REFLECTION

_____

_____

_____

_____

_____

_____

_____

_____

_____

_____

_____

_____

_____

_____

REFLECTION

_____

_____

_____

_____

_____

_____

_____

_____

_____

_____

_____

_____

_____

About the Author

My name is Linda K. Henderson. I have three daughters and five grandchildren. My husband and I have been married for 45 years in October. We have lived in Paducah, Ky and raised our children here. We enjoy our Rocky Ford MBC family. Thanks for your support and prayers. Since Mini Messages from God came into existence, I have had book readings, libraries, and other events, spoken at churches about the books, shared my journey with Podcasts and attended many vendor events. I am looking forward to new experiences as the Lord leads and the satisfaction that comes with sharing and leaving behind a legacy of faith in God. God Bless.

Contact info: E-mail
lkhendesign@yahoo.com

My books can be found on Amazon, kindle, and venues where books are sold.

More Books by Linda K. Henderson

www.ingramcontent.com/pod-product-compliance
Lightning Source LLC
Chambersburg PA
CBHW071220160426
43196CB00012B/2362